Defrosted Gems

Joan Ashe Hagans

Defrosted Gems

Library of Congress Control Number: 2021913167

Printed in the United States of America

Printed - ISBN:978-1-7354872-6-7

Published by:
Sonship Publishing House Inc.
www.sonshippublishing.com

Edited by:
Nova Walton-Marriott
Hier Self, LLC
www.hierself.com

Cover Design: Vanessa Johnson of Vanessa Johnson Enterprises

For my children Eric, Joavan and Joshua
You are my gifts from heaven. Never stop dreaming....

For my husband, Charles
The best human being I know. Never stop believing....

To my mother, Flora Ashe and my father, John Ashe
for their never-ending love and support.

To my sisters, Mary, Sandra, and Mildred, I
am better because you love me.

To Aria Skye and Jéveon Jashan, Grammy loves you dearly.

To Jevel, Amber and Mykhal, I'm so glad you're family.

To Sarah and Melinda, you are my lifelines.

To Veverlyn and the sisters of Women of Wisdom #38,
Order of the Eastern Star, thank you for encouraging
your Associate Matron to shine bright.

The rough terrain of the frozen tundra can be seen as a beautiful winter wonderland, filled with precious stones, if one changes his or her perspective. Similarly, the way we choose to view a situation determines our experience. When we shift our thoughts from negative to positive, we can begin to see the gems in our rough terrain.

I once used the term "defrosted gem" to describe anyone in my life who had the ability to be a blessing to me but chose not to. I helped so many of those same people and I could not understand why no one would help me too. I was unable to comprehend the coldness. I felt cheated and hurt each time I encountered an obstacle they could have helped me avoid. I became weak and withdrawn at the thought of their rejection.

My perspective changed when I recognized some of the most beautiful and resilient things in nature have periods of weakness. We must undergo a slow growth process to meet our full potential. The essence of human nature is to emerge more powerful from a helpless state. For example, the butterfly cannot skip the stage of being in a cocoon.

Whatever your challenge is, please learn to respect the refining process. You must be willing to be honest about your frailties and disappointments. Exposed in one's reflection, sometimes the tears must flow; the fear must show. The mirror doesn't lie. Know that it takes incredible strength to show weakness.

Positive thoughts helped me understand that my poems, not people, are the defrosted gems. They have been frozen for many years, but the sun is shining. I'm so happy to finally be able to share them with you.

Defrosted Gem

I am all woman, but sometimes I feel like a girl,
I've been in a shell, but so has a pearl.
I am very courageous, but sometimes I'm shy,
I've been in a cocoon, but so has a butterfly.
I give my heart, but protect my soul,
I've been forged by fire, but so has gold.
I appear very strong, but sometimes I'm weak,
I have crumbled, but so have mountain peaks.
I've been disappointed, but that's the way it goes,
I've shriveled up, but so has a rose.
I had a dream, but it was only mine,
It slipped away, but so has time.
I'll get some sun, but when I shine,
Stay where you've been, defrosted gem.
I've been really cold, but winter is through,
Spring has blossomed, and I have too.

Written by Joan Ashe Hagans

We are intricately connected to those on our life's journey. Unbeknownst to us, we may affect lives with which we have no formal relationship. It may be the smile you shared with someone who felt isolated that serves as confirmation that they are not invisible. Your vibrant energy may have reminded someone that life is a celebration. These qualities are natural. They are not often thought of as gifts, except to the recipient.

Deep within us we possess the power to heal and validate one another. It is important we do not selfishly deprive others of our truth, wisdom, or honesty. The lessons that life teaches us become keys that can unlock closed minds and open spiritual doors for others. In our truths lie freedom and love.

I have lived a rather blessed life thus far. It has been speckled with great joy and pain. I have generously shared the joy and have been told I inspire others. As I have found ways to remain positive through adversities, I've freely shared my triumphs. What I have been selfish with are the stories of my passage through painful situations. A great deal of those experiences are exposed in my poetry.

Until now, those poems were kept private because allowing them to be read meant exposing that I had become weak at times. The reader would then know that something or someone had gotten the best of me. I wasn't ready to reveal that I had been defeated more than once. But recently, I shared a poignant poem with a dear friend. I was surprised to discover that while our lives weren't duplicates, there were striking similarities. It was liberating to finally discuss it with someone who understood. It was through that conversation I was able to release my social inhibitions and this book was written.

I encourage you not to ignore your innate abilities, your gifts. Be brave enough to offer your contributions. You are more powerful than you know. Someone is waiting for just what you have to give.

This could be your testimony…

Many gifts have been received,
From a force as strong as yours,
Your truth, wisdom, and honesty,
Have allowed spirits to soar!

Someone smashed a
brick wall down,
And exposed a broken life.
Someone told the ugly truth,
That kept them up at night.
Someone found a voice again,
And sang an honest song.
Someone wrote what they
could never speak,
With no fear of being wrong.

Someone broke hate's
inhibiting chains,
And danced their way to free…
Someone took a giant leap,
And let love be the key.

Someone boldly faced a fear,
And laughed at a personal flaw,
Someone left their comfort zone,
And challenged the self to more…

Someone composed a heart song,
Equipped to meet with pain,
So that healing, curing, salty tears,
Could make them tough again.

Someone strutted down
Main Street,
Head high and proud to be,
Someone God had fearlessly made,
Phenomenally…

Someone met themselves
face to face,
And truly chose to live,
Empowered by your
works and words,
Because you chose to give.

Written by Joan Ashe Hagans

If ever there were a time to keep your head down and remain focused, it's when you are striving for greatness. There is no way to predict how long the race will be. Ahead of you lies rough terrain and unchartered waters. Your stamina will be tested. At times you will stumble and fall; you can't keep score.

The very ones you expect to be your cheering section will become naysayers. Don't let this discourage you. To achieve greatness, you must summon uncommon fortitude. You will undoubtedly have to use the fire in your belly for fuel. At your lowest point, when you are inclined to quit, push harder because you could be on the cusp.

A cusp is a point of transition. It's the state in which everything changes.

Weariness has entered my psyche and made me feel as if my efforts would be defeated. But the human spirit is invincible when driven by purpose. I rest in assurance that there is a higher power that will bring me to my destiny even when I can't see how. This power is accessible to us all. Our job is to just keep trying.

On The Cusp

If I would record how many times I'd fall,
I would never get up at all.
If I took time to think about giving up,
I might quit when I'm on the cusp.
If I'd count how many tried to hold me down,
When I'm gifted, I would never be lifted,
I know if I keep on trying, I will reach my mountaintop,
So, I'm never gonna stop,
And I know if I keep believing,
I'll be living every day,
Just like I've been dreaming.

Sometimes it gets hard to see,
Just how to reach your destiny.
That thing, you know, that's burning deep inside,
It's your place your paradise.
Naysayers come and haters go,
But don't give up when you're on the cusp.
I know if you keep on trying, you will reach your mountaintop,
So, don't you ever stop,
And I know if you keep believing,
You'll be living every day,
Just like you've been dreaming.

I know that I just can't stop,
'Cause I am on the cusp of something,
I am on the cusp of something good.

Written by Joan Ashe Hagans

Most individuals believe in their talents, they only hope that others will. Belief in oneself is the proverbial bird in the hand. Hoping would figuratively be the two birds in the bush. Hoping is intangible and there is no guarantee you will acquire what you hope for. What you believe can be manifested.

We were born with everything we need to fulfill our true purpose. We arrive here sure of it in our souls. Doubt is not instinctive. We absorb that negative energy from our surroundings. Our exposure to other talented people causes us to draw comparisons. We slowly become less confident in our greatness.

The road to one's destiny is not an easy one. Traveling is not for the faint of heart. One must stay focused on the vision and never quit, even if you slip and fall.

I certainly know how it feels to be blessed with a gift and still question if I'm good enough. Doubt reminded me that I was fifteen credits short of my bachelor's degree AND never had any professional training. Of course, without proper credentials no one would ever take me seriously. Surely love and passion would not be enough. My dream, the vision of my soul, was dying. To remedy this, I drew from the well of faith. Dreams live where faith abides. I am now a living testimony of what holding on to your vision can do. Thankfully, I took pride in my heart's push for one more try. I now have a DREAM TEAM of professionals in my corner. It turned out, I had what I needed all the time.

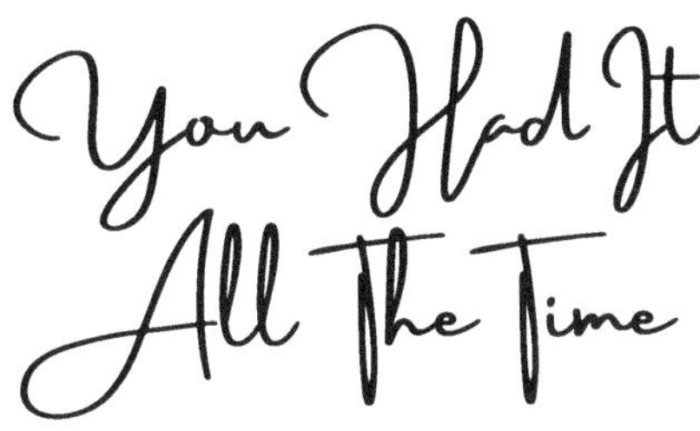

Believing is one bird in your hand.
Hoping is two birds in the bush.
Faith is the water in
your wishing well,
so your dreams won't ever run dry.
Throw caution to the wind,
so you can find your strength within.
Faith won't let you lose your grip,
but if you slip, pull up again.
Take a leap of faith,
Believe in what's inside,
You had it all the time.

Hold fast to your dreams,
they are the visions of your soul.
Without a soul, you're not living.
You will be empty 'til you're old.

Throw caution to the wind,
So you can find your
strength within.
I promise you, faith won't
let you lose your way,
but should you feel lost,
find courage instead.
Take a leap of faith,
Believe in what's inside,
You had it all the time.

Even when your mind says quit,
your heart says one more try.
Take it all in stride,
and never lose your pride,
keep your dreams alive.
If life is but a dream,
then choose to dream now...
Believe in what's inside,
you had it all the time.

Written by Joan Ashe Hagans

The quiet beauty of snowflakes almost immediately transports to me a magical place. An inexplicable excitement fills my heart with whimsy when it snows, even if I'm not in the best mood. Watching each unique snowflake fall until the hard ground is covered in a sparkling blanket of softness pauses life. For that period, there is stillness. In those moments, a cleansing of my corner of the world is divinely occurring.

I love snow. A walk in the falling snow brings me peace. Snowflakes dance to the music of the wind and greet my face in a frenzied rhythm before they take a final bow. Similarly, most of my troubles have been short-lived. They have come in like a whirlwind and quickly melted away.

The footsteps of many travelers are recorded in the snow. Those anonymous footprints are proof that someone else has passed that way. It's comforting to use that concept as a metaphor for life. We all must travel pathways alone sometimes. It is important to remember that we are not the first and will not be the last to navigate through challenges.

I can't stop smiling as I watch children absorb all the wonder of snow. They aim to fall as they make angels, snowballs, snowmen and even snow cones. They pause to enjoy the miracle. In our lives we slip and fall and sometimes have trouble getting up on our feet and starting again. Isn't it amazing how we take it in stride if we fall on the snow? We laugh at our inability to always keep balance. We accept that getting up is not always easy. We must lock that in our spirits when the snow disappears.

The snow soon loses its beauty as we clear away the magic and modify the crystal-like covering so we can go about our lives. I encourage you to hold on to the joy found in the fleeting presence of snowflakes.

When your world seems like an awful place,
You can't always run and hide,
But it seems to have a whole new face,
When snowflakes fall outside.

Suddenly everything is so bright,
You can let your troubles fly,
And see things in a whole new light,
When snowflakes dance from the sky.

The worries you thought were here to stay,
That so often make you cry,
Suddenly seem to go away,
If a snowflake hits your eye.

You can go back to childhood,
When you didn't have a care,
Laughter can do your heart such good,
When there are snowflakes everywhere.

Lock those feelings in your soul,
And never forget how it felt,
To let faith in the good times take control,
When the snowflakes begin to melt.

And when not even a trace of it can be found,
And your world is back in place,
Whatever comes to get you down,
Imagine a snowflake on your face.

Written by Joan Ashe Hagans

I sat on a bench, on a perfect spring afternoon, under a grove of pink flowering trees. I was tired from working mandatory overtime and under a bit of personal stress; not that anyone cared. I had decided no matter how busy I was, it was time to use my gifts. I was spending several hours per week in a recording studio, in addition to running my household and working a very demanding job. This quiet time I decided to take realigned my thoughts and burdens seemed insignificant. For amidst worldly chaos, the earth responds to Divine Order. The overwhelming feeling of being out-of-sync is overcome when we witness the miracle of Spring.

We like to think that we run our lives. We create or agree to our daily schedules. At times, we do a poor job of time management and when we fall short of our responsibilities, we feel inadequate or defeated. That day I learned that relinquishing that power to the Creator and living according to His plan for my life was the key. Nothing happens before its time. The new blades of grass I saw came on schedule. The bushes, that were bare the week before, waited for their time. The breathtakingly, beautiful pink blossoms I admired knew they'd soon give way to green leaves. The earth abides by the law of the Creator, and so must we. Our plans must suit His schedule and not the other way around. Following His lead, we can experience the joy in the bird's song and the lightheartedness of the children playing circle games in the square. We, too, can be in sync.

I gazed upward at a flawless blue sky. There was so much distance between the bright sun and me, yet I could feel the warmth on my face. Surely, the force who set off the "alarm clock" for nature could do a better job with my life than me. That day, I decided to have patience and wait for my season to bloom.

The greatest miracle to behold
I say, without mistake,
Is to feel the warmth as it ends the cold,
and watch the sleeping earth awake.

The ground, once bare is vibrant green
with grass and flowers everywhere,
Trees stand tall, proud, and serene
with countless fruits to bear.

Mother bird sings sweetly in the breeze
after flying north from south,
Finding sustenance now with relative ease
to feed baby's hungry mouth.

Magical laughter fills the air,
The music for the dance,
Of children in the center of the square
while others await their chance.

His majesty, the sun, shines bright
to make the day a little longer,
And if clouds try to steal our light
he shines a little stronger.

The sky is blue, without a flaw
like one never-ending sea,
And sitting way below, in awe,
Is God's thankful creation, ME.

Written by Joan Ashe Hagans

After the same routine day after day, the same scenery, the same four walls, it is natural to yearn for something new, exciting, and different. A long trip usually fits the bill. I felt that way and went to the other side of the world. I had never flown past the International Date Line. You cross over and lose a day! I was so excited! With great friends to travel with, I set off for a trip that would carry me to New Zealand, Australia, and Dubai. I could hardly wait to leave.

I could not have asked for a better trip. I met amazing people, some of whom will be part of my life forever. The majesty of the mountains was indescribable. There were unique species of trees, animals, and birds. My gasps brought in the cleanest air. Everything my eyes could see appeared to be in high definition. I've never seen landscapes so beautiful.

I was blessed to meet and befriend wonderful people who shared their culture with me. I learned a few words in the Maori language. I tried new foods, wines, and desserts. I attempted to learn new dances. Many hours were spent learning about how life is in the various countries my new friends were from. I vow to return for a personal visit with them. No doubt, my excursion was all I longed for and more.

But never did I think I would begin to miss what I had become so bored with. The truth is, the heartstrings are tied to home, wherever home is. There is a human need for belonging. I guess the test of love is distance. I don't regret one moment of traveling so far and the feeling of being foreign. I satisfied my appetite for adventure. Most of all I gained a fresh appreciation for the same routine day after day, the same scenery and the same four walls…home.

The Excursion

Bored by things familiar, predictable, and safe,
My entire being was dying to get away.
I longed for an excursion,
An adventure in a brand-new place,
Where not a soul knew me or recognized my face.
I flew for many hours, so long I skipped a day,
To the other side of the world,
For a very long stay.
The scenery was beautiful,
Perfect as a fairytale.
Mountains so breathtakingly magical,
I thought my heart would fail.
My palate danced the night away,
As did my weary feet,
I learned words in other languages,
From different people I would meet.
I took deep breaths of this strange, new air,
Dipped my feet in the waters clear,
Then something about the ocean's foam,
Suddenly made me long for home.

It's no crime to want adventure,
To escape from your routine,
But make it a short stay, no matter where you play,
For home is where the heart wants to be.

Written by Joan Ashe Hagans

Sound is to the ears what colors are to the eyes. Both have the power to evoke emotions. While colors affect the mind, I believe sound reaches the spirit. Music is the color of sound that affords an otherwise monochromatic spirit to vividly experience emotions.

Music has masterfully colored the canvas of my life. So many songs immediately bring memories to mind. Whether happy or sad, they chronicle special times and major events. As a musician, music is therapeutic for me. I have played chords that were as relaxing and refreshing as eight hours of sleep. Music is essential to set or change my mood. It has helped me celebrate and mourn. In each case, the song connects me to its writer. All aspects of the human experience are shared. Songs confirm that. I write songs knowing that someone else will feel what I feel and believe what I believe.

Each life has a soundtrack composed by human beings who had like experiences and were inspired to set them to melodies. The voices and instruments capture a complete emotion where words sometimes fail. For example, the organ often does the crying for the broken-hearted saying goodbye to their loved one. Each note transcends verbal expression and speaks only to their hearts. It coerces a sense of acceptance and peace. Songs heard that day will forever memorialize a life well lived.

We commemorate birthdays and special holidays with familiar songs annually. They become family traditions. Frankly, without the music we love, our lives would seem empty and feel incomplete. We would lose a very special form of communication. Without Christmas carols, great dance tunes or love songs, we would just be existing. Music is life. There is no life without music.

Life Without Music

How empty would a final goodbye
be if we couldn't hear an organ cry?
While we attempt to quiet our souls,
Releasing loved ones to the new
realm where they have gone?

It would be difficult to celebrate,
The joyous returns of our birthdate,
Without an up-tempo ditty or two,
Shared with those of whom
our hearts are fond.

What would the commemoration
of great joy to the world
be without the familiar carols
while the Christmas tree twirls?
Without jolly melodies
playing all through the day,
As we come close to our beloved
and strengthen our bonds.

I wonder if the aroma would
even smell the same,
In the backyard, in summer,
the grill and the flame,
If there were no rhythms
or sing along songs,
Steadily riding the laughter
and the sounds of the pond.

The peace of a hymn; the
comfort it brings,
The connection to heaven
when the choir sings,
The spirit can worship
and shake itself free,
As soothing chords heal hearts
with a touch from beyond.

What of lovers' memories
of when they first met?
Their first kiss or embrace; the
night they'd never forget?
With no beautiful ballad to recall,
How special it was in the
beginning as time goes on.

Life without music would be
a black and white scene,
Oh, the color that music can bring,
The soundtrack from christenings
to when a man takes a wife,
Life is music, and music is life.

Written by Joan Ashe Hagans

Trees are not concerned if you're watching them; they just are. The complete purpose for their existence is to be what the Creator designed them to be. There's no jealousy amongst them; not one fancies itself more beautiful or more important than the other. They know the Creator makes no errors. Everything touched by the Author of all things is magnificent and meaningful.

People have varying reasons for their fondness of trees. Some have a type of spiritual connection while others simply admire their beauty and mystery. Others acknowledge the physical characteristics; the perfect imperfections that make each one unique and beautiful. Trees, in their silence, teach a lesson of acceptance. They stand stoically with their crooked branches and worship nature with every wind that blows.

My prayer is that women internalize the lesson of the trees. Women have become so self-conscious. We strive to be society's version of perfect. We feel judged if we are not well endowed in areas of our bodies. We constantly change our hair. Some of us seek to alter our skin. Our self esteem suffers if we are unable to bear children. We even dread the blessing of growing older because of the physical changes our new season may bring.

The same perfect designer that created the tree, created us. Each of us are perfect in His sight. He will sustain us in all areas of our lives if we trust Him. We, like the trees, must stand in all our power; grateful for just being.

The Lesson Of The Trees

Every single tree I see,
is beautiful to me.
Though they vary in size and shape,
they reflect God's majesty.
Each one stands their
ground with pride,
countless though they be,
nature's imperfections
only add to their beauty.

Every leaf is different.
They continue to change and grow.
They worship God with
their existence,
With every wind that blows.

Trees trust the Master
to sustain them,
As the seasons change,
They know that life is a cycle,
They do not think it strange.

Some are fruit bearing trees,
others flower: some are bare,
Frost and lack of pollination
can alter what's innately there.

But every single tree I see,
is beautiful to me,
Those imperfections
don't diminish their quality.

I pray that women learn,
the lesson of the trees…
be unapologetically who you are.
Know that God, in His wisdom,
sent you here a perfect you,
although you may think
that you're flawed.

All of His creations,
bring Him honor in their way.
May we be grateful, like the trees,
and accept that we're okay.

Written by Joan Ashe Hagans

Selflessness is an admirable quality. To have a heart for other's needs is rare and sorely needed. I lived much of my life this way. There are many who have learned it is better to give than to receive. The personal joy felt, cannot be measured. It can become addictive. Humility and nurturing allow others to grow. They are attributes that, indeed, make the giver a better person. To watch someone who might not have otherwise ever walked in the light, shine is its own reward.

Years later, I have learned that TOTAL selflessness comes at a heavy price. I have been totally selfless while raising my children and I have no regrets. Children deserve a first chance before you get a second chance, unless both can be accomplished concurrently. However, repeatedly emptying your vessel to fill others is draining. Letting people proudly take credit for your creativity allows them to block your light. You can impede your progress attempting to push others. Simply because you know your strengths and do not require validation does not mean you should relinquish your power in the name of diplomacy.

On matters of the heart, one must find a partner who is equally yoked. A relationship is, at least, a two-hundred percent venture; each bringing his or her total self. ***You will damage yourself attempting to be a person and a half or settling for half of a person.***

Mistreating, neglecting, or depriving yourself, God's best creation, is to love yourself last.

Total selflessness is a sin and, THOU SHALT NOT SIN!

The greatest sin that there can be,
Is loving everyone else,
More than I love me.

Written by Joan Ashe Hagans

I had all but given up on my dreams. I couldn't see how it would ever be possible to accomplish any of my goals. Amazingly, I made peace with it. I knew I had three beautiful children with very special gifts. They would be my success story.

I questioned how I would motivate them. How could I honestly tell them they could do anything and be anything, when I had given up? I could never lie to my children, nor could I be a hypocrite. I searched for the words I would say to them. I could not find any true words. It required remembering who I was. Years before I wrote this quote, "On life's journey, there are no dead ends, only detours".

It was then, I decided to set new goals within reach. I became a licensed Life Insurance Agent. My job afforded me the opportunity to become a certified Instructor of General Topics in New York State. F.E.M.A. has also certified me as an instructor. I obtained a Mental Health First Aid Instructor's license. I began writing for others. Probably the greatest of all, I became an Eastern Star. Serving others is most honorable. Although my accomplishments were not part of my original dream, my children never saw a quitter. Now I am back to pursuing the dreams I almost gave up on. This book is one of those dreams.

Please, never count yourself out. Stay busy and never lose your desire, even if you must take a detour. You will get back on your path. Love yourself and your babies will be proud of you. Teach them that they can fly and be the wind beneath their wings.

Hypocrite

If perchance my dreams must die,
How will I teach my babies they can fly?
How can those words go past my lips,
without sounding like a hypocrite?
I can't say now, but fear I must find,
Something to say, create some line,
To explain why some can have their dreams and others can't,
And that they are in the "can" percent.

Written by Joan Ashe Hagans

After the sixth consecutive night of three a.m. feedings, I often wished my infant could, at least, crawl. As the mother of three, there were many times I wished my babies were born feeding themselves and sleeping through the night. It was the innocent, sleep deprived wish of a weary body. I worked the midnight shift for my entire career to be sure I was home with my children during the day. Maternity leave meant I could be in my bed every night for a brief while.

Before having one child I wanted ten. I have immense love for children. My aim was to fill their days with happiness. But even a labor of love can tire you out and I decided that three children were enough. Motherhood is one of the most beautiful blessings in life. We improve ourselves to set good examples for the lives that God entrusts us to mold. We learn as many lessons as we teach. I learned to cherish each stage of their development. I had to become more patient because time does not crawl, it flies.

Seemingly overnight, we take our babies to kindergarten. We cry at the doorway of the school because we don't want to leave them. A few birthday cakes later and they leave us without a hug. Bottle up the memories before the candles blow out. Those precious years will be gone with the wind.

Challenges come when our children are becoming individuals. We instill values and try to prepare them for the world we know is not as kind as we are. There are disagreements and struggles along the way laden with mixed emotions. Love will always win. Love yourself even if you make mistakes. We will never be perfect. Always do your personal best and you will have few regrets. As they grow and the clock ticks at hyper speed, we start to realize those three a.m. feedings really weren't so bad.

Swiftly your pre-teen will graduate from high school. You will notice he really does look like his uncle once he has a mustache. Your little princess will trade in her glitter for make up to take to college. Then your loves find their loves. In time, you'll cry in the doorway as you wave goodbye, and they go…home.

Cherish each day as a Mom, beginning with the sunrise, because the sunset comes much too quickly.

To Moms

Moms, while you raise your little ones,
At least once you'll wish that time speeds by.
But, oh, my dears, I must warn you all,
Not to blink your eye.
Say your prayers daily,
In good times smile, in hard times cry,
But enjoy each stage of your child's life,
For time begins to fly…
And then, like me, you'll look around,
And wonder how your "babies" grew so fast,
You may even wish you'd done just one more
Fun thing in the past…
It seems that with the sunrise,
From the very last sunset,
Your "babies" are grown,
Standing on their own,
And time won't have slowed down yet…

Written by Joan Ashe Hagans

A discerning eye can spot valuables hidden in plain sight. Those with limited sight could easily bypass priceless jewels. So, it is with people. It can be puzzling trying to figure out why some undervalue us. With all we have to offer, it seems we are often underestimated and overlooked. When you know your worth it becomes impossible to settle for less than you deserve. No matter the circumstance, knowledge of self refuses to be shortchanged and is determined to wait for one with a discerning eye. It makes no difference if a jewel is totally intact or fragmented, the sum of its parts is still of great value. With proper care, a person who has weathered many storms can be just as beautiful as before the rain began.

Like the teacup, events in life can cause you to shatter. An awakened woman, while desiring to be truly loved and valued, will wait. She will no longer compromise her happiness. She knows in the wholeness of self-love, romantic love is possible. In time, she can be healed and usually, when she least expects it, she will be found and finally "seen".

A Little China Teacup

A little china teacup,
Treated like cheap glass,
Dropped carelessly to the ground,
A million pieces—fast.
Parts did stay together,
By strong will and one sweet dream,
That one day a man would fill it,
Not with curdles, but with cream.

The little china teacup,
All alone and in the dust,
Still wished and wished
for just one chance,
To quench somebody's thirst.
It wanted to feel warm inside,
To be held in two strong hands,
To be the first thing reached
for in the morning,
To be part of someone's plans.
To be needed again at midday,
When the day was at its peak,
And to be the last thing
someone touched,
Before they went to sleep.

The little china teacup,
Could not believe the day,
A tall, strong, handsome man,
Came and swept the dust away.
When he saw all the pieces,
He smiled as if he knew,
They were pieces of china,
And he bonded it with glue.

With love and care he held it
In a place close to his heart,
And vowed not to ever let
his teacup fall apart.

The teacup now feels priceless,
Though the cracks and
chips still show,
The tender love and care it gets,
has let that teacup know,
That even when you're broken,
Your value can still show through,
But it takes a special kind of
man to notice it in you.

And when he handles you with care,
Like you've always dreamed of,
It fills you up, you're warm inside,
And that feeling is called love.

Written by Joan Ashe Hagans

The involuntary smile. The feeling of being invincible. The powerful energy that makes you feel like you can be anything, A new attitude that makes you walk taller than before. The boosted confidence. The rarity of finding genuine kindness, respect, compatibility, and attraction in one intelligent person with an easy way about him. You're in love. Love is so unpredictable. Many would say that's part of the magic. It's as if you are the answer to the other's prayer. Sometimes, as perfect as it seems, the timing is not right.

I tried to *"unlove"* someone before. I never understood how that love had even developed. The worst part, I was already in a relationship. It had gone bad, but I lacked the courage to leave. I knew I should have set myself free so long ago. If I had, I would have been available to fairly explore this new love. I acknowledged that my failure to end my relationship had cost me dearly. Even with no guarantee the new love would last, my heart still wanted the chance to try. I could only win. Either I would really find true love, or I would be alone, at last.

As hard as it was, I knew the best decision was to walk away. My heart was ready, but my life was not. I cursed my indecisiveness. The only thing I knew for certain was I couldn't pull anyone else into my ball of confusion. So, as hard as it was, I ran away.

Months and months passed. I avoided all contact with him. I tried to forget everything about him. I simply could not break the hold. It was as if I was assigned to him. It felt as if he had made a powerful prayer request for me once upon a time and changed his mind. No matter what I tried, I still felt connected, so I asked him to *"unpray"*...

Unpray

Un-pray that prayer you prayed,
however long ago,
That God would send someone to you,
who would love you more than you know.

Un-ask for the one who would want to be,
in your life until you're old,
Un-wish for one who would only see,
your good, your heart of gold.

Un-want Him to send you a friend,
who only wants the best for you,
Un-call on Him, for He answered and,
it's too hard for me to do,

Please un-pray your powerful prayer,
until you really want what you will receive.
Please un-pray it if you really care,
So my heart and mind can be released.

Written by Joan Ashe Hagans

Very few things can compare to the gift of fresh flowers. When I am fortunate enough to receive them, I carefully cut the stems and arrange them perfectly in a fitting vase. It is common for me to temporarily rearrange settings in the home to find the perfect place to display them. The goal is to find an area where they can thrive for as long as possible. With proper care and sunlight, I sometimes forget they are on borrowed time. The once closed buds open and reveal their beauty. Tending to them becomes part of a daily routine, but in time, the petals begin to fall.

In younger years, I had relationships that could be compared to a bouquet of flowers. I sought to find love that was real. I longed for the fragrance, color, and natural beauty of love in my life. Just as a bouquet, my new love became a focal point that brightened my spirit and the space it occupied in my heart. It, too, was an opportunity to bring something real inside. Human nature caused me to prune my love interests, attempting to save only the "good parts", plucking out one dead thing at a time. While I did my best to nurture it, the inevitable was waiting to happen.

My lesson was, not everything beautiful is meant to last. The beauty of youth is to receive the bouquets. Enjoy them for what they are, as long as they are. Never try to prolong their existence. Accept the joy it brings you and when the time is expired, let it go. You will undoubtedly receive several bouquets. When you do, remember, there are no roots. Learn to care for them and retain that knowledge. In time, you will bring beauty inside, with roots. Lovingly plant them and watch them grow.

Bouquet

You were it…
The gift I dreamt to receive,
You were the best I had ever seen,
Too good to believe,
You even smelled good; you deserved a special place,
I made room so you had the perfect space.
If I was feeling a little down, your presence brought a smile to my face,
You opened and began to bloom,
You lit up my gloomy room.
And there I was planting a love garden,
Watered it every day,
Tending to my love garden,
Taking care in every way.
Here I was sowing a love garden,
But you were a bouquet…
Beautiful, but dead when I got you…

Written by Joan Ashe Hagans

For all of life's ills, a smile is the best elixir. However, happiness does not always originate internally. Sometimes you must draw from the external beauty surrounding you and borrow a smile. This has been my life's practice. Knowing no one in sorrow smiles, I've used smiling to generate happiness.

I suppose it all began by observing those who seem to be devoid of happiness. Many times, they have drained mine with their expressions. Most complained and never had a good word to say. Their misery wanted company, and they'd make everyone feel as dismal as they were feeling. Subconsciously, I decided I would always spread happiness with a smile.

This strategy seems to work. I smile even when my personal circumstances are nothing to smile about. I simply shift my focus to things in nature that have retained their beauty no matter what. The world has always been filled with ugliness, yet the negativity never steals the sun's shine. Therefore, I refuse to let the battles of life or love steal mine. A smile can cover pain or sadness like the shade of a tree in the heat of the day. This does not mean that in solitude I don't allow myself to feel. I'm just determined not to be a killjoy to others I encounter.

Simulating happiness is most difficult when my heart is heavy. I have so much free love for people and often, it seems difficult to even give it away. On days my borrowed smiles are met with blank stares or rolling eyes, I wonder if I've only fooled myself. It's a very lonely place to be.

Waking up to see any new day, no matter what it brings, is true happiness; push through. Walk expecting joy and I promise, along the way, you will be met by happiness and be able to genuinely smile.

Fake

It's a good thing the sun is beautiful,
Within its warmth my smile is free.
For God leaves no one with nothing,
He lets the sun shine just for me.
And until I have some sunshine of my own,
I'll smile in the rays He sends my way,
Never gonna see me feeling sorry for myself,
'Cause the sun comes up every day.

It's a good thing trees are beautiful,
There are many trees lining my way.
They all stand tall and strong in the rain,
Cold strips them bare and they start again.
So, until there's someone to cover me,
I'll smile and stand beneath their shade,
Never gonna see me falling to the ground,
When rough winds blow, I'll just sway.

So tired of asking the question,
Why I'm full of love that I can't share,
I'll put on my smile and walk each lonely mile,
and let happy meet me there.
I'll show up smiling every day, just like the sun,
But like a tree's limbs I could break,
There is no one under the sun, who'll know my smile is fake.

Written by Joan Ashe Hagans

In each of our minds is a "trunk" where we preserve and honor our most precious thoughts and memories. Not every pleasant experience earns being saved. Only the dearest, most special ones that touch the core of our souls can permanently exist there. As life continues, we hopefully have new special encounters that will soon be tucked away.

In pensive moments, we unpack the trunk and momentarily bring life to past joys. We become engulfed in the warmth of loving days gone by. We give thanks for the people and the things that have enriched our lives. Growth allows us to laugh at the silly things and we honor the serious lessons we have learned.

We seldom meet someone who we value enough to share our treasures with. When we do, we believe that it is safe to let that person in. The level of trust given to such an individual is rare. How sad it is, then, to find that they were not fit to know the intricacies that make you who you are. They have the potential to taint that which is pure and must be removed.

Thankfully, my discernment has not allowed me to let many enter my sacred space. I fell prey to one pretender who seemed worthy. At first, it felt sincere when he inquired about things that touched my spirit. What I shared with him barely scratched the surface, but I was quickly disturbed. He attempted to control my thinking. It became clear that he only wanted to learn my vulnerabilities so that he could manipulate me. Once someone knows what moves you, they have power.

Beware of those who only pretend to love you; the ones who want to go too deep, too fast. Do not ignore your feelings of doubt. We are all blessed with the gift of discernment. We must let it guide our decisions. Don't rush to reveal the essence of who you are. Had I given him full access to my inner thoughts and memories, I could have relinquished my peace and joy. Instead, I purged my "trunk" of him and preserved all that is precious to me.

My Trunk Is Junky

I have a very special trunk,
Where I keep my precious things…
Pictures and notes from loved ones,
And graduation rings.
Reminders of my early childhood,
Memoirs of my teenaged years,
Journals and diaries,
Documenting smiles and tears.
Stuffed animals who became "family",
Pressed flowers from young "true" loves that died,
My first Bible, handmade gifts from my kids,
All neatly tucked inside.

I trusted you and let you into,
The treasures of my life,
The sum of all you've added to me,
Is pain, deceit, and strife.

Of late, my trunk is junky.
Your rubbish does not earn,
A place among my memories,
So, it's been removed and burned.

Written by Joan Ashe Hagans

Some people don't value valuables. If life has bestowed the riches of health, stability, family, and friends on them, they often take the blessings for granted. Those who never experience rainy days believe sunshine is a given. However, it is baffling how those who have endured tumultuous storms can be oblivious to their fortune.

Many seek the treasure of love. While it is so easy for some to give love purely and wholly, it is not always recognized as precious. Consequently, the dear one who has freely given such an invaluable gift has it rejected.

I experienced such cavalier treatment by my first true love. I struggled to understand how it was so easy to walk away from a beautiful new family, knowing so many were in search of what we found. It was clear to me that I had not lived enough to have such wisdom. Thankfully, I had people in my life whose experiences far exceeded mine. Through wise counsel I learned such poor decision making was not mine to own. I could not let it change me. I was assured I would encounter someone more discerning and deserving. I knew my value. I did not fall. I pushed on knowing it was not my loss.

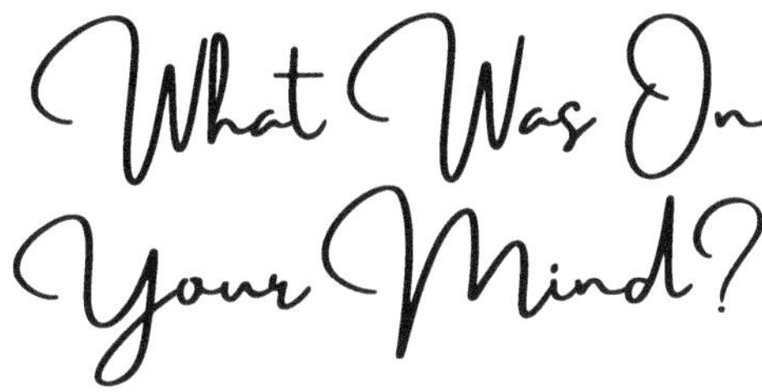

There are people looking everywhere,
for someone who will really care.
And there are many who'd give anything,
for one moment of the joy real love can bring.
Love that doesn't need a reason.
Love that won't fade throughout life's seasons.
And if they found that kind of love,
they would never let it go,
because they'd know,
how hard it is to find today…
So, what was on your mind,
when you threw your gift away?
You had love as pure as rain.
And it's your loss, I'm telling you it's your loss,
'Cause I don't think you'll ever be loved this way again.

Written by Joan Ashe Hagans

This poem is the lamentation of a broken twenty-four-year-old wife and mother. At seventeen, I was an innocent, inexperienced church girl who followed the rules. I vowed to wait until I was married before I was intimate with anyone. But in my senior year of high school, I met a seemingly respectable young man who also went to church. He had a beautiful family that I still love dearly. Soon, I had broken my promise. I felt like the lowest human being on earth. I thought if we eventually married, I could absolve my sin.

We went to college and barely survived the four-year long-distance relationship. There were so many signs that we would never have a happy marriage. Yet, a year after he graduated, we married. I prayed that God would accept my human sacrifice and bless our union.

A year later we had a perfect baby boy. While on a year's leave from work to care for my son, I had a devastating revelation. My loving family had been keeping a secret from me. My husband had expressed interest in a family member. Of course, it was one sided. I wished I had followed my instincts and left him years before. Now I was a wife and a mother. According to my beliefs, ending my marriage would be another sin. So, I forgave him, but I never, ever forgot. Before my maternity leave was over, he was having an affair with someone at work. I prayed. I cried. I was afraid of the repercussions, but at last I had had enough. I made an appointment with an attorney and demanded that we begin divorce proceedings.

I felt totally disconnected from God. I didn't feel worthy to go to church. I stopped singing. I was a shell of myself, and it led me further and further away from everything I believed in.

For every church girl who is desperately trying to live according to the teaching of the church, please hear me! You ***do not*** have to stay with someone who does not respect you under ***any circumstances***. Pray for forgiveness if you believe you have sinned and ***leave***! God is love and He knows your frailties. He will not condemn you. Do not condemn yourself to a miserable life. Give him back to the world.

Giving You Back To The World

Found the man I'd been dreaming of,
The perfect man on earth,
That's when my heart gave birth to love.
We took vows side by side,
For me, it meant forever,
I thought nothing could sever,
The knot we tied.
Our love created a brand-new life,
Someone we could raise together,
As a family brave the stormy weather,
But a little rain came between this man and wife.
Now you want to separate,
Think there's something new to find,
Your love is truly blind,
If you think that it's too late.
My tears alone could save the roots of this family tree,
But the only thing standing here is me,
'Cause you left me on my own.
I'm hurting deep inside,
Excuse me while I mourn,
But the love that was born has died.
I'm no longer your pearl.
So here I sign on the dreaded dotted line,
As I give you back to the world.

Written by Joan Ashe Hagans

Saying a final goodbye is never easy. Life often forces us to do hard things. Whether it's time for a bright new beginning or an end to darkness, goodbyes are always difficult. Each life is changed forever at the sound of goodbye. Lives are no longer intertwined. The future is altered due to the absence of someone who has been relevant in your life.

Divorce was the goodbye that pushed me to start anew. Almost instantly, I felt the true weight of womanhood. I was suddenly, solely responsible for my son's future. There was no one to rely on for child support. Not the kind the court orders, the kind that God ordains! I felt each move I made had to be right EVERY time. There was little to no room for error. How could I handle my commute from Westbury to Manhattan, work at night and still be the attentive mother my son deserved? Could I find and afford a suitable, closer place to live? Who would babysit? That was incredible pressure. I thought I would fail, but I knew I couldn't.

This life change was swift and drastic, but necessary. In the blink of an eye the word goodbye had changed my dreamy future. You know, the one where I'd live happily ever after? I stood alone facing the uncertainty of reality but reimagined my story. I began to visualize being happy on my own. I learned to ask for help. I harnessed the strength of my motherly instincts. Most importantly, I forgave. My transition was now smooth because I held no malice in my heart. I sincerely wished him the same happiness I sought and prayed life would not change his smile.

Goodbye

Time goes by so swiftly,
You just blink your eyes,
And things that change forever,
Sound as simple as goodbye…
Goodbye changes time, changes minds, changes lives…
Goodbye, my love, I hope that time is kind to you.
If we should meet again,
I hope time won't change your smile.
Don't let nothing change your smile,
Goodbye.

Written by Joan Ashe Hagans

A few words etched into an arched stone will one day, briefly sum up our lives. They will not tell a complete story. Those who gaze upon the stone will only know your name, birthdate, and date of expiration. Perhaps, it will state whether you were a beloved woman or man. Even those who knew you well will never know your entire story. Only you know that.

What if you were to project your epitaph? Today, if you were to compose a final statement, how would you describe your earthly experience? I believe you would discover that your accumulation of material things and stature in life would not be included. A full life is measured in intangible quantities. The amount of happiness, faith, kindness, and love one possesses are the only considerations when determining quality of life.

Consider the life of a woman who has a kind heart. She loves her neighbor as herself. Her life is spent trying not to hurt anyone, especially her partner. This woman sacrifices her happiness attempting to repay a sacrifice once made for her. Attaining real joy for herself means misery for him. So, she lives an unfulfilled life and endures undue heartbreak and loneliness. She justifies this by convincing herself it is the right thing to do. As a result, the comfortability she affords him eludes her. She is ultimately kind to everyone but herself. But her faith assures her that she will be rewarded for her sacrifices after life. Her projected epitaph is that of a fool.

I have spent a great portion of my life living the story of our fictitious woman. Unfortunately, I know there are countless others. Fortunately, it is a story that can take a positive turn here in the land of the living. We must never injure ourselves to spare others. We must always choose personal happiness. It is unfair to deny ourselves life's precious intangibles.

I took a vow to ensure a positive synopsis of my life. I will live in the abundance of those intangible things. My projected epitaph is, "She learned to love herself". You may write that in stone.

Epitaph

On her tombstone was inscribed,
"Here lies a fool",
Who lived her life for someone else,
So she wouldn't be called cruel.
She accepted a life of loneliness,
To show her gratitude,
To someone who rescued her once upon a time,
She didn't want to be rude.
Just another sad story,
Like countless others underground,
Who, like her, lacked the courage,
To reclaim her heart from the lost and found.
Hopefully, reincarnation is real,
And whenever she returns,
I wish her love that she can feel,
An eternal flame that burns.

Written by Joan Ashe Hagans

Sometimes we must walk alone. Solitude is a time to become centered. However, if we're not careful, we may wander off the trail and find ourselves lost. If we are distracted enough, we lose our sense of direction and can't find our way home. In unfamiliar territory when we feel isolated, we should stand still. Many of us continue to stray so far from the Light we become spiritually disconnected.

A spiritual disconnection leaves the heart barren. You may thirst for human companionship, but only to fill empty spaces. In that state, your choices will take you in the wrong direction. If you choose someone who does not feed your spirit, you will still be in the desert of your life. Your soul will still be thirsty.

As a very young woman, I rejected the idea that I needed anyone. I had been hurt and lied to and felt I would be better off alone. I would be the center of my attention. I would supply my needs. I wanted no phony friends and no fake relationships. I secluded myself. Even Sunday worship was no longer a part of my master plan. After all, what good had it really done? The easy thing to do was accuse God of leaving me. Soon I was embarrassed to reach out to people I had put off and I was too ashamed to pray. I learned the difference between being alone and loneliness. ***To be alone is to move away from people. Loneliness is to move away from God.***

We must put to rest the part of ourselves that separates from spirit. Then in the stillness of the morning we will be able to hear the voice of true love. God is love. ***It is never He that leaves us, we wander off.*** His love is an oasis in the desert. His love is the compass that leads us back home.

Is your heart an empty field,
a weather-beaten ground?
Are you standing lost amidst barren trees,
with no one else around?
Tired of the loneliness you feel,
how much you want to be found...
How your heart must cry in pain,
and never make a sound.
You long for sweet companionship,
for a place that feels like home…
Has your hope for love abandoned ship,
like all the people you have known?
Wouldn't it seem just like a dream,
if you woke one morn from sleep,
to find a slow, but flowing stream,
where still waters run deep?
If you could feel a warm breeze in the air,
and from the same direction it had blown,
a still, small voice whispers in your ear,
that you've never been alone?
Take comfort, then, and know that God is always in control,
Even in the desert of your life, He's an oasis for your soul.
He is an ever-loving friend, a confidant indeed,
He'll give you an abundant life,
And all the love you need,

Written by Joan Ashe Hagans

When we are well, our mind, body and spirit are unified. We follow our intuition. We do not allow anything to disrupt our peace. Everything is in sync if we honor ourselves. Wellness is a very delicate balance. The spirit must be protected if we are to remain whole.

Our natural gifts are of the spirit and are to be honored as well. I was blessed with the gift to sing and write beautiful songs. I met a producer and he felt there were more opportunities in Atlanta, Georgia. He moved first and called me soon after with the news that I had been signed to an independent label. My biggest dream was coming true. I was so excited! We agreed to move from New York to Atlanta. I recorded a 12" single called "My Life". Then my life totally changed. I was expecting a baby. I chose to leave so my, then, husband could return to New York for a job in his field. I deferred my dream for his. I did not honor my gift or my opportunity. I could have stayed in Atlanta and raised my son. Within ten months after his birth, I was alone. I refused to sing for at least the next ten years because the hurt was too deep. This was the first blow to my spirit.

We live in a physical realm, so the mind and body are naturally very powerful. The mind is motivated by the desires of the heart. It is the spirit that needs nurturing to remain strong. So, we must be diligent with our quiet time, be it prayer or meditation, to remain in tune. If we neglect it, our spirits are in danger. Over time your mind will make decisions based solely on the emotions of the heart.

Because I was no longer in tune with my spirit, my heart did whatever was easy. After a great deal of turbulence, my heart sought peacefulness. My heart needed a normal, quiet life. From a new relationship I had a beautiful daughter. Sadly, this relationship ended abruptly due to his substance abuse. This all but killed my spirit. Yet, my heart refused to stop trying, but it was losing its fight.

Then, came the calm. A perfect gentleman who thought he was in love with me. Soon I had my third child. Our son was his first child. I had the things I thought I needed. My heart let that be enough. But it truly wasn't enough. My partner and I lived together but alone. I wanted, needed, and deserved more. I didn't make demands when I was displeased. I feared upsetting our very stable life. I did not believe I could survive any more turbulence. So, I played it safe and as a woman, I died.

I have now been retired for two years. The children I didn't even have when I started are all grown now. I find myself with a lot of that quiet time I mentioned. Recently, I heard my spirit again. It's still strong although it was silenced. My spirit cried for all the needless pain my heart let me endure. I urge you to never smother your spirit.

Going forward, I will be guided by my spirit. I have some tough choices ahead of me, but my spirit won't lead me wrong. I wish you WELL.

Waterworks

My heart let my spirit cry today,
For all the painful years,
That it has forced it to stay strong,
By holding back the tears.

For telling it "tomorrow",
For promising "next year",
By requesting just a little more time,
While it lived in selfish fear.

For making a free soul play it safe,
For taking away the air,
For settling for less love than it deserved,
As long as someone cared.

For letting dream thieves smother and steal,
The gifts that God placed there,
The heart let the mind soothe its conscience,
As if the spirit wasn't there.

Ten, twenty, thirty years,
The heart refused to share,
Decisions with the spirit,
And it simply wasn't fair.

So, my heart let my spirit cry today,
But no vows did it make,
Since the heart has seen its failures,
I wonder what new steps it will take.

Written by Joan Ashe Hagans

Tributes

I am not perfect, but three times in my life I got everything right.

To carry children is to learn what it truly means to let God use you. You must place complete trust and relinquish all control to the Creator. Miraculously, another life grows within you. Your knowledge is not required. You are simply a vessel. Intuitively, you learn when to move and when to be still. Patiently you wait for His work to be complete. A perfect creation is born of that total surrender.

I am blessed to have three miracles. I recognized them as such and quickly dedicated them back to God. My children are the continuous good, beauty and joy in my life. I cherish the day, the hour, and the minute that each of them was born. I love every quarter inch of them. That God found me worthy to mother them leaves me speechless. I pray that I've prepared them to touch the world with their special gifts and virtues.

My task was to love, nurture and inspire them. More importantly, to teach them to honor the life force that brought them to me. All my children are adults now. Each of them has taught me valuable lessons. Eric taught me courage and perseverance. He has been with me through lifechanging transitions. He is loving and strong. Joavan is an extraordinary woman who is wiser and braver than I ever was. Her love is immense and fortifies me. She has taught me grace and acceptance. Joshua is unconventional. He does not easily conform. He has great faith and loves deeply. He has taught me patience and flexibility.

I am not perfect. I have not done everything right, but God used me perfectly three times.

My Miracles

(Eric, Joavan & Joshua)

ERIC

At 2:46 on a Wednesday morn,
My first child, a son was born.
Though it was thirty-three years ago, I still remember,
That wonderful day, the 14th of September.
At 19 inches the perfect little boy,
Was a 6 lbs., 10 oz. bundle of joy.
Nothing had ever been so great!
It was the main event of 1988!
The most wonderful thing I had ever done,
Was giving birth to my precious son.

JOAVAN

I thought that there could be no more joy to the world,
Until I saw my little girl.
It was a Thursday at 6:50 am,
I felt all those wonderful feelings again.
6 lbs., 10 ½ oz. of sugar and spice,
Made August 13th especially nice.
A 19 ¾ inch angel made her debut,
On planet earth in 1992.
Twenty-nine years have passed and she's more beautiful now,
And she's even sweeter, though I don't know how.

JOSHUA

I'll never know until I get to heaven,
How I was blessed again in 1997!
With yet another handsome son,
Born on Good Friday, what a precious one.
It was March 28th, and he got a quick start,
Stealing his piece of my heart,
7 lbs., 8 oz. of love and joy,
All in a 20 ½ inch baby boy!

I looked at him and knew why I was alive,
That evening at 8:35.
It's twenty-five years later and I'm still in awe,
Of the beautiful baby whose eyes I saw,
When he first got a glimpse of me,
Now I wonder what they all see.

I hope they've seen pure love in my eyes,
As I've grown with them, and to my surprise,
I've learned so much from them over time,
I love them and I'm so glad they're mine.

Written by Joan Ashe Hagans

My mother is the embodiment of love. Love emanates from her like the most pleasant scent from a flower. She is bathed, sun-kissed and saturated with goodness. Her name bears witness, Flora.

She is everything a mother strives to be. Home was a safe place where each of us could be unique and flourish. It was immaculate and beautiful. She could paint, lay flooring, and fix just about anything. Our environment was always peaceful and secure. Our lives had consistency and structure. She lived by the values she instilled in us. She demonstrated what is best in human beings daily. Love was felt in everything she did, even her discipline.

We tasted love in our nutritious meals and delicious cakes baked from scratch. We felt love in the pretty garments she made for us. Even our teddy bears were meticulously made with love in every stitch. She sketched us every few years to perfection. With the polished voice of an angel, she sang meaningful songs while she played our piano. I find myself singing a lot of her favorite hymns when I need grounding.

I loved to hear Rev. Flora Ashe preach as well. Though a beautiful and dainty "flower", she was boldly helping to build the kingdom. She officiated many weddings, christenings and funerals with such poise and grace. She has been retired for some time but believes she will preach a message of wisdom and love at least once more. Her strong faith made us confident that all things are possible if we believe. I know I always have a compassionate listening ear, sound advice and loving arms to hold me when I'm down. Mom is now eighty years old and is as beautiful and loving as ever. I thank God for allowing her to be here. She's the best Mother, Grandmother and Great- Grandmother any of us could ever ask for. Flora Ashe is my Mother and she is exceptional.

Flora

(My Exceptional Mother)

Soft as a whisper and strong as the wind,
named for the flowers your beauty transcends,
mortal sight and carnal minds…
You are love personified.
Sunshine that brightens the darkest of times,
wisdom that guides and brilliance that shines,
love that has swaddled me since my life began…
You are my Mother, my teacher, my friend.
Calm that has silenced the storms in my life,
peace that has pulled me through struggles and strife,
Joy that has lightened my very soul,
Life gifts more precious than emeralds or gold.
Arms that have been the only safe place I've known,
Gentle as summer rain—and now that I'm grown,
I appreciate you more as time passes you see,
Nothing compares to my Mother and me.
As certain as I am that there will be a new day,
I know that your love will never burn away.
No one alive is more blessed than I,
Flora Ashe is my Mother, my gift from on high.

Written by Joan Ashe Hagans

Every child needs a hero. They need good qualities to admire. As parents, where they find their hero lies heavily on you. The people, places, and things we expose our children to will heavily impact them. Children are impressionable and influenced easily. Parents please be careful to keep your children in an environment where they can find a positive hero. Sometimes their hero may even be you.

My Daddy is the most intelligent person I know. He has done amazing things in life and been justly rewarded. He provided for his family. We had all we needed and a lot of what we wanted. But the most precious thing he gave me didn't cost a lot of money. This wonderful man gave me his time and his full attention. He is my hero.

He cleverly taught me about life sitting at an old bridge table in his den. There we would play checkers and chess. We listened to the best music of the 60's and 70's. This may not sound special to you, but we would have sardines with mustard, crackers, and ginger ale. It was our special snack.

Playing our games, I learned to think ahead. He had me think about the consequences of each move. I was warned not to move too fast. Daddy never let me win, I had to earn that. I was taught to stand up for myself. Fear was not entertained. I had to try to beat whatever or whoever it was. If I tried my best, a loss was never a total loss. Whenever I needed him, he was always there. He made sure I knew my thoughts and opinions mattered. My confidence was solid, and he always let me know I was important. This is the power of a father in your life.

Excellence is still the goal when it comes to My Hero and me. God has blessed me to still have him here rooting me on. I've never had a total loss; I just keep trying my best. Daddy thinks I'm special. It's still all that really matters.

My Hero

(For Daddy)

Sardines, crackers, and ginger ale,
A card table in the den,
Checkers, chess, and good music,
Memories from way back when.

I learned to give life all I had,
That trying my best
meant I couldn't lose,
Lessons I learned spending
time with Dad,
When I could barely tie my shoes.

Those times were very special,
I felt like a big girl,
My opinion counted,
With the smartest man
in the world.

He answered a million questions,
Although I asked a million and two,
For the others he handed me a book,
To find my answers, without a clue.

I was raised to be a tough little girl,
Small things couldn't get me down,
If there was ever something
I couldn't handle,
I knew my hero was around.

As the years went by,
I had my share,
Of failures and wondered why,
But from the lessons
learned in that den,
I always had the strength to try.

Fathers, know your impact,
Its importance can't be told,
Your every word and action,
Fortify the soul.

Other's negative opinions.
Never shook my confidence,
My Dad thinks the world
of me, and I of him,
And it's all I've needed,
then and since.

Written by Joan Ashe Hagans

As a child, loneliness was something I never experienced. I'm blessed to have a sister who is sixteen months younger than me. Her name is Mary, my little Mary. Together, we went through all the insecurities and fears of growing up. That was outweighed by the fun and constant companionship that sisterhood brings.

Our parents instilled strong values and beliefs in us. I would describe our upbringing as wholesome. Mary and I made the most of every moment of every day. We shared a room and dressed alike even when we didn't have to. We rarely argued until we were older and began to cook and wash dishes.

Adolescence presented us with normal challenges, but we felt no pressure to follow the crowd. We knew we would not stand alone following our convictions. As a result, we were able to live blissfully in the innocence and beauty of being young girls.

For the most part, we attended the same schools and shared the same friends all the way to college. We had help finding ourselves, leaning on each other. We were inseparable. In time, we branched off to live our separate lives. Mary is brilliant and I knew she would be fine. I married and moved away but returned. Later, she married, moved away, and started a new life in a new city.

Parenting and demanding careers left little time for visiting. My heart soon became familiar with loneliness for my little Mary. I'm so grateful for our early years filled with lasting memories. I can simply pause and recall one of our precious times and realize she's in my heart and never far away.

Many hot, summer evenings, just after dusk, we would play in the backyard. Armed with a jar with tiny holes punched in the lid, we set out to catch fireflies. We had lots of practice getting over "the one who got away". It was fun but exhausting work. Through teamwork, we would eventually fill the jar. The strange, green glow from the jar became our light for the night. We shared secrets and dreams until we fell asleep.

Our lives are now less demanding, and happily, visits are more frequent. I still have many days when I miss my "little Mary", so I merely close my eyes and remember us.

(For My Sister, Mary)

I often miss the strange, green glow,
From a jar in summertime,
Earned from many hours of labor,
Catching fireflies.

Such a calming "nightlight",
Dazzling to the eyes,
Proof of an evening full of fun,
Before we came inside.

Giggling with the lights out,
Our pajamas were the same,
We'd share our dreams and wishes,
Before the Sandman came.

Of course, we said our nightly prayers,
Before we fell asleep,
A heartfelt plea was for my sister,
I prayed the Lord, her soul to keep.

We traveled much of life's road side-by-side,
And soon, as grown women know,
The time came to chase our passions,
And like fireflies, set a glow.

We live so many miles apart,
But to feel close, I merely close my eyes,
And recall the long, hot summer nights,
When we caught fireflies.

Written by Joan Ashe Hagans

My "Idol" is not famous. She is not rich or showy. She is very unassuming. Nothing about her is loud. She possesses a quiet strength I have always admired. Ironically, if you asked her, she would tell you a very different story. She views herself through a lens colored by her experiences. I doubt she realizes that, even through her struggles, she has inspired her younger sister all her life. This powerful woman is my sister, Sandra.

Situations that would have broken most women have only made her more determined. She is fiercely independent. I have never heard her complain. She only prays that she continues to find a way to make her way. She has often been isolated by the ignorance of those who didn't take the time to understand her. She holds no grudges, nor does she speak ill of anyone. She understands the power of words and does not use them to tear anyone down. She has such inner beauty.

Her beauty is not limited to her heart. God created her with a goddess in mind. She has every physical attribute any woman desires. She is not conceited. She is not self-absorbed.

When faced with ups and downs, rarely did she reach out. She met her challenges head on and sometimes got bruised. Her injuries were only to herself. Her sense of humor has allowed her to laugh when most would break down and cry. She possesses the power to overcome anything, and I pray she knows it.

This is the declaration of a proud sister who has admired the strength, stamina, and optimism of a woman who is one of a kind. For all my years, I've tried to imitate Sandra's qualities. That has served me well. She has inspired me like a big sister should.

My Idol

(For My Sister, Sandra)

Your beauty is a certain thing,
Though poetically we're told,
That the perception of beauty,
Is left to them who behold.

Yet, unanimously a flower,
Wins the nod of all who gaze,
You, too, like the flower,
Have been beautiful for all your days…

Beautiful, not only in spirit,
But in physicality,
In your sense of humor,
In your solidarity.

The model strength that you display,
Prompts one to self -evaluate,
My sister, in case you didn't know,
I wish I were so great.

Never doubt your beauty,
Or your strength to overcome,
You've always been my idol,
I've never found a better one.

Written by Joan Ashe Hagans

In the span of a lifetime, you may receive an award for a lauded act or use of a talent or skill you have honed. It begins with a dream that incites your determination to work extremely hard to reach that pinnacle of success. It is human nature to desire recognition for your merits. If fate is kind, you become what you desire.

Though I sang all my life, it wasn't until college that I believed in the possibility of singing professionally. A music career would have been my ultimate joy. I seemed to make all the right connections at the right time. Before I knew it, I was signed to an independent label, and everyone was excited by what we thought would be my career. I was ready to work tirelessly and earn my Grammy award. I had visions of it.

But life had other plans. Instead of laboring over my music career, I veered off into motherhood. I viewed this as a detour, not a dead end to my musical dreams. I was blessed with the gift of a child. I knew I had done nothing to earn that.

I have shared many stories with you that span my lifetime thus far. My detour has certainly taken me on the scenic route. Those mountains, valleys, and winding roads led me to a comfortable place called home. My three children are now grown and two have children of their own. They each have a special love for music. Life offered me more than ***awards***. For my hard work as a mother, I received my grandchildren, Aria and Jéveon as ***rewards***. They are unquestionably my ultimate joy. If fate is kind, you become what you so desire. I am now called Grammy.

Grammy

I once desired a Grammy since they told me I could "sang".
I eagerly awaited what the coming years would bring.
Like a fish in water, where there was music, I was "me",
I thought singing was my ultimate joy, certainly my destiny.
Life's highway had a detour that put me on the "scenic route",
Far away from lights, makeup, and dark, padded sound booths.
Soon I had a family with three children I have raised,
Each of them music artists, Ms. Different, Josh-O and Haze on Haze.
Grandchildren, Aria and Jéveon; they're all ultimate joy to me,
What I desired, I became; I'm proudly called, **Grammy**.

Written by Joan Ashe Hagans

I uttered a prayer that my shaken faith did not believe would be heard. After two failed relationships, I felt enduring love was meant for everyone but me. This was not a pity party; I had had heavy doses of reality. I was afraid to choose anymore. The love I was searching for would have to find me. Heaven would have to intervene and send me an angel.

Heaven smiled. My easy kind of love came in the form of a friend. Someone who I had deep respect for. However, nothing would be easy about our decision to be together. This friend was the friend of my ex. We had never had any romantic feelings for each other in the past. I am being candid about this because someone reading this might be in this situation. They may reject someone special due to the opinion of others. It wasn't comfortable but having a truthful conversation with our common friend turned out to be the key.

Before we realized our friendship had changed, he did some remarkable things. He singlehandedly saved a Christmas. He walked over a mile in 10 ½ inches of snow to bring me a gallon of milk and went directly back home. He always called to make me laugh. The sound of birds chirping would remind us that we had talked on the phone all night. He knew all that I had been through. He encouraged me and assured me I would be alright. His actions showed me I was in his heart. Intuitively he knew what I needed. I valued his friendship and truly hoped he'd find someone who deserved him. Thankfully, my prayer caught this angel's wing.

My angel was a divine gift sent to my children and me. His love tore down the survival walls I had erected. Loving him was effortless. My life was suddenly peaceful, secure, and stable. To watch him with the children blessed my heart. He brought them so much joy. He was so attentive and loving. There was no pressure or unrealistic expectations, but I knew we would have a child together. It was twelve years before we married. Crazy, but I finally felt safe. This poem is actually a wedding song. I am telling this story twenty-six years later. Taking the chance was the right thing to do.

An Angel's Wing

I'd been praying all my life,
for someone to love me for me.
And I waited all this time,
wondering if heaven had heard my plea.
My prayer caused heaven to sing,
it caught an angel's wing, an angel's wing…
brought you down to me,
and I found everything I ever dreamed in you.

You're the love of my life.
Never imagined I'd feel this way.
We'll share our lives,
watch our babies have babies,
we'll grow old and gray.
My prayer made heaven sing,
it caught an angel's wing, an angel's wing…
sent you down to me,
now I have everything I'll ever need with you.

Time has come and gone so fast,
I just know our love will last…
And I know that we've been blessed by heaven's open smile…
My prayer touched heaven's heart strings,
It caught an angel's wing,
My everything,
You.

Written by Joan Ashe Hagans

About The Author

Joan Ashe Hagans was born and raised in Brooklyn, New York. She recently retired from the New York City Police Department Communications Section, where most of her thirty-year career was spent as a Training Instructor at E911. She is certified as an Instructor of General Topics by both New York State and FEMA. Joan is also a New York State licensed Life Insurance Agent. She attended Brooklyn College.

Her parents had all girls. They are a very close family. Her sisters have since relocated to southern states, but Joan and her parents still reside in Brooklyn. Having grown up the child of a preacher, Joan is both spiritually and socially conscious. Her genuine love for people causes her to be very involved in community projects. She strongly believes that we are here to freely serve others. She is currently the Associate Worthy Matron of Women of Wisdom #38, Order of the Eastern Star. Universal Supreme Council of the Thirty-third and Last Degree, Inc.

Joan began writing poetry at a very young age. Poetry became a way to chronicle the joy and pain of her life. She is also a songwriter and had a very brief music career in the 1980's. She continues to create music and lends an ear to her three children who are all musically gifted. Family is everything to her. She is overjoyed to have two grandchildren and they have shown early signs of being musically inclined.

For twenty-five years she has had the love and support of her husband, Charles. Each of them is very proud that she has finally realized the dream of sharing her poetry with you.

www.ingramcontent.com/pod-product-compliance
Ingram Content Group UK Ltd.
Pitfield, Milton Keynes, MK11 3LW, UK
UKHW020422250726
13967UKWH00007B/2765

9 781735 487267